The Author's Gold Rush

How to Harvest a Bountiful Crop Repeatedly

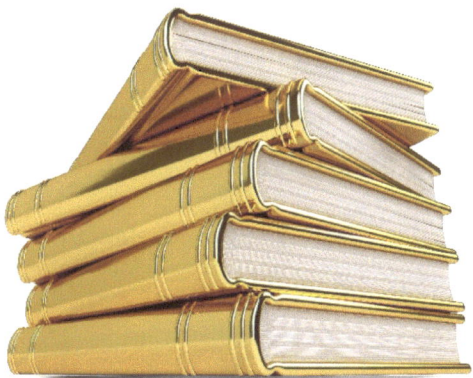

Kim Staflund

The Author's Gold Rush
How to Harvest a Bountiful Crop Repeatedly

From the author who brought us

Successful Selling Tips for Introverted Authors praised as
"...a critically important instructional reference -- especially
for reluctant, bashful, or introverted authors."
by Midwest Book Review, Jim Cox Report

and

How to Publish a Book in Canada recommended as
"A good source for writers of all experience levels seeking to
publish quality books in Canada."
by Kirkus Reviews

Kim Staflund
Polished Publishing Group (PPG)

The Author's Holy Trinity of Profit (Book Two)

The Author's Gold Rush: How to Harvest a Bountiful Crop Repeatedly
Ebook ISBN: 978-1-988971-36-0
Paperback ISBN: 978-1-988971-37-7
© 2019 by Kim Staflund

🍁 PolishedPublishingGroup

Due to the dynamic nature of the Internet, any website addresses mentioned within this book might have been changed or discontinued since its publication.

For authors:

"During the gold rush, it's a good time to be in the pick and shovel business."
~Mark Twain

The Author's Holy Trinity of Profit **Trilogy**

Action
The Author's Money Tree: How to Grow a Bountiful Readership Organically

Thought
The Author's Gold Rush: How to Harvest a Bountiful Crop Repeatedly

Faith
The Author's Magic Key: How to Stay on Track and Keep the Faith

TABLE OF CONTENTS

INTRODUCTION

In book one of this trilogy, *The Author's Money Tree*, you learned how to plant, grow, and harvest a bountiful readership. Book two, *The Author's Gold Rush*, is a simple business system that can be repeated daily. You can use it to harvest that same crop again and again with ease.

Information is Your Gold Rush

As we discussed earlier, you could be in any room chatting with your family members, friends, or business colleagues. It doesn't matter where it is or who you're with. At some point during the conversation, a question of some sort almost always arises; what's the first thing everyone does? You each pull out your smartphone, iPad, or tablet and open the web browser to search for an answer to that question. We all have instant access to timely information at our fingertips now, and we're all constantly accessing it.

People are looking for *your* information online, all over the world. Non-fiction authors and subject matter experts (SMEs) need only share that same information with a growing number of readers. Hook them by offering them something of value that makes them want more, and they'll be your fan for life. I'll show you how two authors are growing their readerships by directing new traffic to their *backlist* books.

Entertainment is Your Gold Rush

This system can work just as well for authors of fiction and poetry as it does for SMEs. Why? Because people are constantly searching for sources of entertainment, inspiration, and tribute online, too. The world is filled with voracious readers looking for a great book series to escape with in their spare time. There are just as many others looking for the perfect poem to eulogize a loved one or motivate a team.

But what good is any of this if no one can find it? Perhaps, this is your current predicament. Maybe you've already written and published a few books online that aren't getting any traction whatsoever. You're lost like a needle in a haystack. This system will ensure new readers are consistently finding all your books *and* your blog. It will help you grow your readership and subscriber base even larger, even faster—like adding lighter fluid to the fire you started in book one.

Relationships are Your Gold Rush

What you do with the readers who find you is the most important step of them all. When you personalize their experience with you and your books, they'll be your followers for life. I'll show you how one of today's top independent authors continues to harvest the same crop of fans again and again by using them as beta readers to help him improve upcoming book launches.

To build a lasting relationship with anyone, you must first build the trust between you. When they see you as an authority on the answers or entertainment they seek online, they'll begin to follow you. When they see you as a *person* they can relate to who truly cares about them as a subscriber and fan, they'll begin to view you as a trusted friend. How you think about them while you're writing for them will make a world of difference to your results.

The Digital Gold Rush

In book two of this trilogy, we're going to cover what email marketer extraordinaire, Anik Singal, refers to as "The Digital Gold Rush" in much more detail. While my advice will be tailoured specifically to authors, there are things Anik refers to in *The Circle of Profit* that apply to all digital marketers:

> You are now going to see the power of building a business based around information. ... There has never been a better time to create this kind of digital publishing business. More and more, people are turning to the Internet for information.
>
> The best part is that these people are not just looking for free information; there are millions around the world happy to pay for it.
>
> I genuinely believe that this is the modern-day California Gold Rush. I'm serious. (Singal, 2016)

It's quite simple. All you need to get started are three things you most likely already have: a computer; Internet access; the ability to write. In fact, if you've already written and published several blog entries and/or books, you're well ahead of the game. Backlist books are an asset in the online world—especially backlist *ebooks*.

The best part is that you don't have to quit your full-time job to do this. You can easily do it part-time. For Joanna Penn, it took five years to transition into a full-time writer. It took another four to earn a six-figure income. Still, it was well worth all her time and effort as she now earns a *multi* six-figure income.

Three Feet from Gold

In Napoleon Hill's revolutionary bestseller, titled *Think and Grow Rich*, he discussed many case studies of people who had failed and succeeded throughout history. Most importantly, he discussed *why* so we can all learn from them.

One of my favourites is a story about R.U. Darby and his uncle that I will share with you here.

> One of the most common causes of failure is the habit of quitting when one is overtaken by temporary defeat. Every person is guilty of this mistake at one time or another.
>
> R.U. Darby, who later became one of the most successful insurance salesmen in the country, tells the story of his uncle, who was caught by the "gold fever" in the gold-rush days, and went west to dig and grow rich. He had never heard the saying that more gold has been mined from the brains of men than has ever been taken from the earth. He staked a claim and went to work with pick and shovel. The going was hard, but his lust for gold was definite.
>
> After weeks of labor, he was rewarded by the discovery of the shining ore. He needed machinery to bring the ore to the surface. Quietly, he covered up the mine, retraced his footsteps to his home in Williamsburg, Maryland, and told his relatives and a few neighbours of the "strike." They got together money for the needed machinery and had it shipped. The uncle and Darby went back to work the mine.
>
> The first car of ore was mined and shipped to a smelter. The returns proved they had one of the richest mines in Colorado! A few more cars of that ore would clear the debts. Then would come the big killing in profits.
>
> Down went the drills! Up went the hopes of Darby and Uncle! Then something happened—the vein of gold ore disappeared. They had come to the end of

the rainbow, and the pot of gold was no longer there. They drilled on, desperately trying to pick up the vein again, all to no avail.

Finally, they decided to quit. They sold the machinery to a junk man for a few hundred dollars and took the train back home. Some "junk" men are dumb, but not this one! He called in a mining engineer to look at the mine and do a little calculating. The engineer advised that the project had failed because the owners were not familiar with "fault lines." His calculations showed that the vein would be found *just three feet from where the Darbys had stopped drilling*! That is exactly where it was found.

The junk man took millions of dollars in ore from the mine because he knew enough to seek expert counsel before giving up. Most of the money which went into the machinery was procured through the efforts of R.U. Darby, who was then a very young man. The money came from his relatives and neighbors, because of their faith in him. He paid back every dollar of it, although he was years in doing so.

Long afterwards, Mr. Darby recouped his loss many times over when he made the discovery that desire can be transmuted into gold. The discovery came after he went into the business of selling life insurance.

Remembering that he lost a huge fortune because he stopped three feet from gold, Darby profited by the experience in his chosen work. His simple method was to say to himself, "I stopped three feet from gold, but I will never stop because men say 'no' when I ask them to buy insurance." He owes his "stickability" to the lesson he learned from his "quitability" in the gold mining business. (Hill, 1937)

You see, there is so much more to your success than simply the **action** plan I laid out for you in book one of this trilogy. In fact, **thought**—both yours and your readership's—will play a huge role in the outcome of your plan, as will be shown in this book about why email marketing is so effective. But, without **faith**, it's difficult to maintain one's positive thinking about any success plan. Isn't it? That's why book three is so important for you to read in conjunction with the others. It is, perhaps, the greatest key to helping you stay on track until you reach your personal goal. It will help you learn Darby's "stickability" without stopping three feet from gold as he did.

YOUR SIMPLE BUSINESS SYSTEM

In the "harvest" section of book one, we touched briefly on the power of email marketing to help you grow your readership online. We also looked at blog subscribers versus registered users—and why you need to build your email *subscriber* list above all else. That list is as good as gold once you learn how to utilize it effectively.

> An email address (if treated properly) is worth a lot of money. It is a true business asset. A value very commonly accepted by information marketing experts is $1 per email address.

> That means that if you can build an email list of 10,000 subscribers, you can generate a profit of $10,000 per month - simply by properly managing that list! (Singal, 2016)

In this book, we'll look at email marketing in more detail including the psychology behind building and monetizing your subscriber base. You've already done much of the work just by writing and publishing your blog entries and books. Now all you need to do is drive more traffic to those webpages.

How to Further Build Your Readership … in Your Sleep

Here are the three primary tools you'll be using to build your subscriber base a little larger each day: an opt-in page; a special offer of some kind; and an autoresponder. Once these are all set up properly, pretty much everything will work automatically in the background for you. This simple business system can be repeated daily, and it can literally bring you new subscribers while you sleep.

Hook Them with an Enticing Opt-In Page

If you want to build your subscriber base more quickly, you're going to need more than just a subscriber widget on the front page of your blog. You're going to want to create a specific opt-in page and promote it in strategic places online.

I recommend leaving that opt-in page off your blog's main menu. Keep it separate from everything else. Whereas other posts on your blog—perhaps even the main template of your blog—will contain links to where your books can be purchased, you aren't going to sell anything on your opt-in page. The sole purpose of this page is to entice people to give you their email address and become one of your subscribers. Period.

How will you do this? For starters, you'll want to keep the opt-in page simple but eye-catching. The main heading of the page should directly appeal to a strong pain or pleasure point for your readers. Here are some examples:

- **Fiction book series:** Love vampires? Then you'll love this!
- **Non-fiction self-help:** Too busy to make healthy, home-made meals?
- **Inspirational poetry:** Boost employee morale with this!

That's it. One line. One compelling statement that speaks to a passionate desire or problem common to your fan base. You should also add an attractive picture directly below or beside that heading for emphasis. You'll draw in more people that way.

Engage Them with a Special Offer

Underneath that heading and picture, you'll want to include one or two short sentences along with a basic Mailchimp signup form people can use to submit their names and email addresses to you. It's nice to get at least their first names so future autoresponder emails can be addressed to them in a more personalized way. But that's all the information I ever ask for to keep things comfortable—just the name, email address, and preferred subscription options.

Here are some examples of additional sentences you can include on your opt-in page:

- **Fiction book series:** Enter your email address to receive a FREE "sneak peek" into book one of the popular vampire series *The Bloody Truth About Vampires*. You'll also receive FREE updates on upcoming book launches and special offers.
- **Non-fiction self-help:** Enter your email address below to receive a FREE ebook filled with healthy meal ideas that can be prepared in less than 15 minutes. You'll also receive a FREE weekly newsletter highlighting other great recipes and special offers.
- **Inspirational poetry:** Enter your email address here to receive five FREE motivational posters for your office meeting rooms. You'll also receive one FREE inspirational quote by email each week to share with other staffers.

When people subscribe, they will receive an email shortly after clicking on the "submit" button to send you their information. (This email is already pre-set in your autoresponder as described in the next chapter.) Within that email, they'll receive the promised gift. There are different ways you can give it to them:

1. First, you can attach the ebook or printable posters as .PDF files inside the automated email. Unfortunately, this makes it a little too easy for them to share the gift(s) with others.
2. So, a second alternative is to include a private webpage link, such as this one, inside the body of that email: https://www.slideshare.net/KimStaflund/sneak-a-peek-9780986486982-publish-a-bestselling-book. This is a more secure place where they can view and/or download the file for free.
3. Or, thirdly, you can include a link directly to your blog where they can find additional links to download the gift(s) from Kobo or Amazon. Here's an example: https://blog.polishedpublishinggroup.com/free-books/. Not only is this a secure option; it can help your author ranking on these ecommerce sites as well as your blog's search engine ranking.

Manage Them with an Autoresponder

An autoresponder is a specialized tool that is used to manage all these emails as your subscriber base grows larger. Mailchimp for WordPress has a free option for lists up to 2,000 subscribers. After that, depending on the service you use, autoresponders generally cost from $30 per month and up to maintain. It all depends on how many email addresses you're working with. By the time you reach 2,000+ subscribers, if you're doing things rights, you should be earning enough additional income to more than cover that monthly fee.

> The email addresses you collect on your opt-in page do not sit on your own computer. They actually fly into a database automatically, using a copy-and paste line of code that you've put on your page. This

database of email addresses is called an autoresponder.

There are many third party companies, which will manage the entire autoresponder process for you. It's incredibly easy. They give you a line of code that you simply copy and paste into your opt-in page. Instantly, the email addresses that your visitors enter are automatically placed into your autoresponder. (Singal, 2016)

You can automate so many things using an autoresponder like Mailchimp. In fact, you can use it to create more than one opt-in page for various types of subscribers—a perfect option for the authors out there who write both fiction and non-fiction, who wish to reach and grow more than one audience. Can you imagine if you had to try to keep all these email addresses straight yourself? It would be so easy to mix them up. With an autoresponder, it's all done for you in the background. The email addresses that come to you through one opt-in page are placed in a different list than the ones that come from a second opt-in page. You can set up different automated email messages and personalized gifts for each list.

Additional automation can be set up using the Mailchimp for WordPress Premium plug-in. For example, if you have a shopping cart attached to your site, and one of your subscribers visits that shopping cart but then leaves it before buying, Mailchimp will send a message to encourage him or her to complete the purchase. Just imagine how many more sales could be completed with this option!

KISS: Keep It Simple, Silly!

I don't want to overwhelm you with too much automation to begin with. It's best to ease in and keep things simple at first. For now, all you must do is this:

1. Install the free Mailchimp for WordPress plug-in to your WordPress blog site. (How to Install WordPress Plugins Tutorial: https://www.siteground.com/tutorials/wordpress/install-plugins/.)

2. Create a Mailchimp account: https://Mailchimp.com/help/create-an-account/.

3. Log into your new Mailchimp account so you can get your unique API Key which is needed to integrate the autoresponder program with your blog. Copy and paste that API Key into the appropriate spot on the settings page of your Mailchimp for WordPress plug-in. (You'll see it when you click on the plug-in to view it.) This tells WordPress which Mailchimp site it is connected to.

4. Enable these three WordPress integrations within that plug-in: comment form, registration form, and custom. What this does is ensure that each time someone comments on your blog, subscribes to it, or supplies their email address through some other custom opt-in page, that email address will be placed into a default list within your autoresponder. You can name that list whatever you'd like to name it. For now, keep it simple and call it "blog subscribers" or something like that.

5. Now, you'll also want to let Mailchimp know which WordPress site to connect it to. You do this by going back into your Mailchimp account and clicking on "Connected Sites" within the drop-down menu under

your account name. A list of various ecommerce sites, website builders, and other options will be displayed on the page for you. You'll find WordPress in the "website builders" section. Click on it there. Type your blog site's URL address into the appropriate spot and indicate that you want all email addresses from this site connected to your "blog subscribers" list.

That's all you need to do for now. Based on all the activities we discussed in book one of this trilogy, you should already have regular traffic visiting your blog. Now their email addresses won't only be listed for you to view in your WordPress admin area; now they'll also be placed within an autoresponder that will allow you to utilize them more effectively. We'll talk about how you can do that in chapter two.

PRIMARY COMPONENTS OF AN AUTORESPONDER

There are so many things an autoresponder can do for you as you begin to grow your readership larger and larger. If you want to dive in deep—to fully understand all Mailchimp's features plus the psychology behind how and why email marketing works so well—I recommend you read Anik Singal's free ebook titled *The Circle of Profit*. A link to it is listed in the Bibliography section of this book. It's one of my online business bibles.

For our purposes here, I want to stick with the basics and keep everything as easy as possible. I'd rather have you spend your time blogging and writing books than writing daily emails or weekly newsletters. So, this book contains the essential knowledge you'll need to get started with email marketing as an author.

Email Lists

There are a few details that, by law, need to be included in all the emails you send out to subscribers. You'll fill in this information by clicking on the **Lists** menu at the top of your Mailchimp screen (the main menu) and then clicking on the email list name itself. Within that menu, you'll see another sub-menu option called **Settings**. Here is where you'll fill in this important information.

List Name and Defaults

Under **Settings**, you're going to choose the **List name and defaults** option if you ever want to edit your list's name. For our purposes here, we'll keep it as "blog subscribers" for now; I just wanted you to see where you can change it. You'll also see some other options here that will help with your security and regulatory compliance.

For example, under **Form settings** I like to check the **Enable reCAPTCHA** box to prevent spambots from adding emails to my list. I also like to check the **Enable GDPR fields** box to ensure I can add fields to future forms that meet with the General Data Protection Regulation (GDPR) regulations related to the data protection and privacy of all individuals within the European Union (EU). This is important if you wish to reach a worldwide audience with your blog and your books.

Under the **Campaign defaults** sub-menu, I like to check all the options: **Send a final welcome email** to new subscribers; **Let users pick plain-text or HTML emails**; and **Send unsubscribe confirmations to subscribers** when they opt out of my list. To create the email, click on the **list forms designer** link within that option. From there, you'll be redirected to the **Form builder** page. This is where you can edit and adjust the various automated forms (templates) that are used to create signup forms for subscribers, automatically send a thank you email to those who have already subscribed, et cetera.

Form Builder (Final Welcome Emails)

To create a personalized welcome email for new subscribers, you'll want to choose the **Final welcome email** option in the **Forms and response emails** sub-menu. You'll see how all the form fields are already populated for you, including the text for the automated email. It will simply say "Your subscription to our list has been confirmed." But I don't just want to leave it that way. I like to personalize things right from the start, including offering free gifts within the email (as described in the last chapter), so I click inside that box and replace the one-liner with this text:

Hi friend,

First and foremost, I want to thank you for subscribing to the PPG Publisher's Blog. I hope you receive tremendous value from the information contained within.

I want you to know I plan to share so much more with you in the coming days, weeks, months ... for as long as you'll stick with me on this journey. And who am I? Why would you want to stick with me? Well, I'm someone who knows a lot about this book publishing, sales, and marketing business—someone who can help YOU to sell more books of your own.

As a bestselling author and TESOL-certified sales coach for authors with over 25 years' experience in the book publishing industry, I can teach you how to publish, advertise, sell, market, and publicize your book(s) using all the effective traditional and online tricks of the trade. Add my substantial corporate sales and advertising background into the mix, and you have a serious mentor in front of you who can help you achieve better commercial success as an author.

That's the business side of things. Now for something a bit more personal ... so you have a better idea of who you're dealing with here. I love to travel! In 2016, I achieved one of my most cherished travel goals by going on what I'll call an "Eat, Pray, Love" working holiday to Asia. This is me: https://www.goabroad.com/interviews/kim-staflund-2016-program-participant

What a fantastic adventure I had! Not only did I visit Thailand, but I also got to see parts of China, Malaysia, and Singapore while I was there. All beautiful countries filled with wonderful people.

Okay, enough about me for now. In the coming days, you'll receive notifications whenever I post something new on the PPG Publisher's Blog. Occasionally, I'll let you know what I'm up to in "real time," too. Cheers to our new friendship!

Until we meet again...

All my best,
Kim

P.S. As an additional thank you for subscribing to the PPG Publisher's Blog, I hope you'll enjoy downloading and reading these free books: https://blog.polishedpublishinggroup.com/free-books/. I'll also make sure you're informed whenever there are other special offers available for you to enjoy.

I want that first email new subscribers receive from me to be friendly and personalized to some degree. I want it to remind them of the value they've just signed up for, but I also want to tell them a little bit about me as a person. That starts to build our relationship right from the start. You'll see the rest of the information at the bottom of the form auto-fills with their personal information, subscription preferences, and an unsubscribe reminder in case they change their mind.

Incidentally, you can create "welcome emails" within the main **Campaigns** section of Mailchimp, too. But I just do it here. And I make sure it is sent out within one hour of the person subscribing to my blog, so everything is still fresh in his or her mind.

Form Builder (Confirmation Thank You Page)

Another form that Mailchimp creates for you is called a **Confirmation thank you page**. It defaults with a simple message that confirms and thanks new people for subscribing to your list, and it includes a **continue onto our website** button they can click on to be redirect to your blog. You can leave it this way if your goal is to increase traffic to your blog. Or, you can monetize this page in various ways. I talk about two of the most effective ways to do this in the affiliate marketing section later in this book.

Take a look through all the **Forms and response emails** within the **Form builder** sub-menu. You may see some other places where you can personalize the automated messages going out to your subscribers.

Required Email Footer Content

Every email you send out must include more than just an unsubscribe option at the bottom. It also has to remind people why they're receiving the email in the first place, and it must include contact information and a mailing address for the list owner (which will auto-default for you). This is required by law. As such, this is the personalized message I use for my email footers: *You are receiving this email because you opted in via the PPG Publisher's Blog. We send occasional special offers as our thank you to you for doing so.*

Google Analytics on Archive and List Pages

If you use Google Analytics to track your blog traffic, as recommended in *The Author's Money Tree*, you'll be happy to know that you can also use it to track your email subscribers through Mailchimp. Simply copy and paste your Google Analytics tracking ID into this spot if you wish to do so. Google will take care of the rest for you.

Create Additional Subscriber Signup Forms

Right beside the **Settings** sub-menu, you'll notice the **Signup forms** sub-menu. This is where you can create more unique email opt-in pages and pop-up forms in addition to the basic subscriber widget that is already included with your WordPress template.

Form Builder

We already looked at two of the options within this **Form builder** sub-menu when I showed you how to personalize your **Final welcome email** and **Confirmation thank you page**. Within this option, you can also build, design, and even translate a unique **Signup form** that can be used to target specific audiences.

Just as you did with that **Final welcome email**, you can personalize the message attached to the form. Then you can share it via your Facebook or Twitter social media accounts. You can even create a special QR code that will redirect mobile customers to your signup form via the QR readers on their cell phones.

Any signup forms you create here will be assigned their own generic Mailchimp URLs (e.g., website addresses). If you prefer to use your blog's URL for all signup forms, for branding purposes, then you may prefer the next two options, instead.

Embedded Forms

When you create a new signup form using the **Embedded forms** option, you can copy and paste the auto-generated

HTML code from that form into the text screen of a WordPress page on your blog. Here's what I mean by that:

Visual Screen

When you're <u>writing a new post or page in your WordPress blog</u>, you'll notice there is a tab for the "visual" screen and another one for the "text" screen. The view on the visual screen will appear as it does in the top indented paragraph, with certain bits of the text **bolded**, *italicized*, and <u>underlined</u>. When you switch to the text screen (bottom blue indented paragraph), things appear differently. Rather than seeing actual bolded/italicized/underlined paragraph text, you'll see just plain text that has what are called HTML "tags" attached to it to. The tags are the background coding that tell the Internet what type of characteristic a particular text element has. What is HTML? **The acronym "HTML" stands for Hyper Text Markup Language** which refers to the structure (e.g., coding, markup) that is used to create a website/webpage.

Text (HTML) Screen

When you're <u>writing a new post or page in your WordPress blog</u>, you'll notice there is a tab for the "visual" screen and another one for the "text" screen. The view on the visual screen will appear as it does in the top indented paragraph, with certain bits of the text <strong>bolded</strong>, <em>italicized</em>, and <u>underlined</u>. When you switch to the text screen (bottom blue indented paragraph), things appear differently. Rather than seeing actual bolded/italicized/underlined paragraph text, you'll see just plain text that has what are called

HTML "tags" attached to it to. The tags are the background coding that tell the Internet what type of characteristic a particular text element has. What is HTML? The acronym "HTML" stands for Hyper Text Markup Language which refers to the structure (e.g., coding, markup) that is used to create a website/webpage.

You're going to cut and paste that code for your newly-created embedded signup form into the text screen of the whichever WordPress page you've decided to use as a signup page. Once you've done that, and you go back to the visual screen view, you'll see the actual form there.

Here's an example of how an embedded form might look on a blog post: https://blog.polishedpublishinggroup.com/2019/03/the-authors-holy-trinity-of-profit/. I created this particular opt-in page using a blog *post* as opposed to a new blog *page* because I wanted it to show up on my Amazon Author Central page through my blog's RSS feed . Doing so helps with pre-promotion of the trilogy on one of the top ecommerce site where my books are sold.

For details on how to set up this kind of syndicated content feed on Amazon, please refer back to *The Author's Money Tree*. In the meantime, you may also want to pick up a copy of my recent *HTML Coding for Beginners* mini ebook from either Kobo, Amazon, or E-Sentral for more help understanding HTML.

Subscriber Pop-ups

You can also use Mailchimp to create special subscriber pop-ups for your blog. No need to copy and paste any code from here into your blog. Simply create the pop-up, then click on "publish" and let Mailchimp do the rest. Since Mailchimp and your WordPress site are already linked together, it will automatically attach the pop-up to your blog for you.

Your pop-up message can say something as simple as "Subscribe here to be first in line for new book release news! You'll also receive first dibs on FREE book downloads and coupon codes for other special offers as they arise." Remember, you want to offer people something of value in exchange for their email address here, just as you would do on any other opt-in page.

Create Email Campaigns to Engage with Your Readers

If you're following the instructions from book one of this trilogy, then you're already blogging and publishing in very specific ways regularly. That's increasing your author ranking *and* search engine ranking which is bringing you more and more traffic each day. That traffic is building your readership and blog subscriber base each day, too.

To ensure most (if not all) of your subscribers are buying your books, it's important to engage with them in a personalized—but highly efficient—manner just like the authors I mentioned in book one. This can be done via Mailchimp's main menu option titled **Campaigns**. There are a variety of campaign options for you to choose from here.

Broadcast Emails (A Monthly Newsletter)

Here is where you can create a monthly newsletter that highlights this month's favourite blog posts/podcasts/videos, upcoming book launches, any other special author events you'll be attending, et cetera. It's also a great place to offer discounts on select books—to let your subscribers know when and where these books will go on sale or be offered free of charge for them only, for a limited time only. A newsletter is intended to broadcast timely, current events to your subscribers; it's meant to remind them that there's a *real* person behind these emails who truly values them as blog subscribers and fans of your books.

When you first set up your Mailchimp account, you'll be prompted to design your first email campaign within the main **Campaigns** menu by clicking on the **Create Campaign** button on the top right of your screen. You'll find a great newsletter template in the default **Regular** section of the **Email** sub-menu.

First, you're going to want to give this campaign a name. (I call mine "PPG Publisher's Blog: Monthly Newsletter" to keep it clear and simple.) Once you've named your campaign and clicked on the **Begin** button, the next screen will appear where you can create your newsletter by adding your "blog subscribers" list to the recipients list. You should also personalize the "To" field with ***|FNAME|*** as opposed to just leaving it generic. These little personal touches make a difference to your subscribers, trust me.

The bottom **Content** portion of this form is where you'll choose whatever template you want to create your newsletter with by clicking on **Design Email**. There are several featured templates to choose from. I prefer the **Tell a story** format for newsletters; it's up to you which template you use.

Mailchimp won't let you send your email to anyone until you've replaced all the placeholder content with your own personalized content. This is a great built-in safeguard. Once you're done creating the newsletter, you can schedule when you're going to send it—whether that's right now, later today, or on another day in the near future. (If you read *The*

Circle of Profit, you'll learn all kinds of tips and statistics behind which days of the week are best for sending out emails and why.)

Mailchimp will take care of the rest and even let you know how many of your subscribers opened the email, how many of the emails bounced due to being sent to invalid addresses, et cetera. You can use this data to clean up your list, from time to time, to ensure it only contains valid email addresses with interested readers in it. Cleaning up will become more important the larger your list grows because your monthly Mailchimp subscription price is based on how many subscribers/emails the autoresponder is managing for you.

Automated Emails (Share Your Blog Posts)

Since your WordPress blog has an RSS feed, you can easily share teasers of your latest blog posts with your email subscribers in the same way you're sharing them as syndicated content on your Amazon Author Central page. You do this by setting up a new email campaign.

First, you'll need your blog's RSS feed link. On WordPress, you'll find a link to it in your META widget titled **Entries RSS** as shown here:

META

Register
Log in
Entries RSS
Comments RSS
WordPress.org

You can click on that link to be redirected to the feed. Or, you can simply type "feed/" after your blog's main URL in order to bring it up. For example, my blog's RSS feed is located here: https://blog.polishedpublishinggroup.com/feed/.

Now, to set things up so that your new blog posts are automatically sent out to your email subscribers, you'll want to go back to the main **Campaign** menu and click on the **Create Campaign** button again. Click on the **Email** sub-menu again. But, this time, you'll want to choose the **Automated** option at the top, second from the left. Here is where you'll find a box that says **Share blog updates** on it. Click on that box.

I like to name this email campaign "PPG Publisher's Blog Updates and Special Offers." You can call yours whatever you want to call it. That name is there simply to remind you what the campaign has been created for. Once you name it and choose your list, you'll be redirected to the next screen where you can copy and paste your blog's RSS feed into the appropriate spot.

If you think your subscribers will be okay with receiving an email every time you write a new post, you can keep the default options as they are. Anik Singal believes the more emails the better, but I think there's such a thing as overkill. Because I only publish up to three blog posts per week, I leave all the default options as they are so that my subscribers are getting each new post in real time; and I send a newsletter once a month to recap that month's highlights for them. I also always personalize the "To" field with ***|FNAME|*** as opposed to just leaving it generic.

Once you click through and choose all your options, you'll be asked to pick a template just as you did for your newsletter. I prefer my blog updates to look different than my newsletter, so I choose a basic text message for these. Whatever template you use, make sure you include these RSS content blocks within the template: **RSS Header** and **RSS Items**. If you leave these out, the blog entries from your RSS feed won't show up in the email. The rest of your content blocks and overall design is up to you.

It's always best to preview and test each email campaign you create through Mailchimp before you save the final version. This will allow *you* to see exactly what your subscribers will see once you launch the campaign. I do this for all of mine. I preview them on my screen; I also send myself an email so I can see how it will look to others. Only when I'm satisfied with these test results do I approve anything for launch.

PPC Ad Campaigns (Facebook/Instagram and Google)

Mailchimp also helps you to create pay-per-click (PPC) advertising campaigns on Facebook/Instagram and Google. What is PPC advertising? PPC is an Internet advertising model used to direct traffic to various websites (also known as landing pages) in which advertisers pay as they go, only when their ads are clicked. It is defined simply as "the amount spent to get prospective buyers to click on an advertisement."

The cost of a PPC campaign depends on a few different factors:

1. Where is it being run (i.e., Google or Facebook)?
2. What region is it being targeted to (i.e., one city, province, or state, an entire country, an entire continent)?
3. How long will the campaign run for (i.e., for a specified amount of time, or until a specified advertising budget has been used up)?

This is a great tool to help you promote your blog and/or books in more strategic places online. When you start a PPC campaign, you agree to pay X dollars per each click on your ads that are redirected to a specified landing page (e.g., opt-in page), your blog's main page, or the ecommerce webpage where your latest book is being sold (hence the term "pay-per-click"). Where Google campaigns are designed to target specific keywords that users might type into the search engine, Facebook campaigns are designed to target a specific demographic such as "female users, age 20–40" or "all users" who have expressed an interest in "book publishing," as two examples.

To create a PPC campaign through Mailchimp, click on the **Ad** sub-menu option under **Campaigns**, then choose either the **Facebook/Instagram ad** option or the **Google remarketing ad** option. Name your campaign whatever you'd like to name it. Perhaps you can call it either "FBI for *Your Book's Title*" or "Google for *Your Book's Title*" to keep things simple.

Facebook PPC Ads

On the next page, you can choose which channel you'd like to run your PPC ads in: Facebook, Instagram, or both. You do this by first linking your social media accounts to your Mailchimp account which is as simple as clicking on each option and then logging into them through Mailchimp.

Mailchimp keeps your next four choices fairly simple and straightforward:
- if you choose "new people" then you can indicate which geographic region, gender, age, and interests you wish to target that are similar to your existing contacts;
- if you choose "contacts" then you can target either an existing Mailchimp list or the list of people who have liked your Facebook page;
- if you choose "custom audience" then you can again

indicate which geographic region, gender, age, and interests you wish to target to find a new audience; - or, last but not least, if you have a paid Mailchimp account, you can also choose to target any of the people who have visited your website, but haven't subscribed to it yet, using Facebook pixels. (About Facebook Pixel: https://www.facebook.com/business/help/74247867 9120153.)

After that, you can choose your daily, weekly, or monthly PPC budget. Then design your ad.

Google PPC Ads

With Google ads, your goal is to bring more traffic to your blog itself as opposed to your social media sites. If your WordPress account isn't already properly connected to your Mailchimp account, you'll be given a bit of HTML code that you'll need to copy and paste into the <head> section of your blog's theme. You will find that <head> section in your WordPress admin menu item titled **Appearance** and the sub-menu item titled **Theme Editor**. From there, you'll see another menu on the righthand side of the screen titled **Theme Files**. You'll want to scroll down that menu until you reach **Theme Header (header.php)** and click on that. The HTML coding for your theme's header section will now appear in the centre of your screen. All you must do is copy and paste the HTML code from Mailchimp somewhere in between <head> and </head> within that main theme HTML code. Then click on the **Update File** button at the bottom to save it before logging back out of WordPress. (Here's a great Mailchimp article with clear step-by-step instructions on how to do this in case you need more help with it: https://Mailchimp.com/help/about-connected-sites/.)

After that, you can choose your weekly PPC budget. Then design five different PPC ad options for your campaign.

For more information about how PPC advertising works on various online platforms, including LinkedIn, you may want to pick up a copy of my recent *Pay-per-click (PPC) Advertising* mini ebook from either Kobo, Amazon, or E-Sentral. It also goes into more detail about how Google Adsense can be used to you monetize your blog.

Landing Page

Mailchimp's **Landing page** option contains the following templates to help you design attractive opt-in pages with specific goals in mind:

- Accept Payments
- Generate Leads
- Grow Your List
- Promote Products

Much like the sign-up forms you create within the **Form builder** sub-menu, any landing pages you create here will be assigned their own generic Mailchimp URLs (e.g., website addresses). If you prefer to use your blog's URL for all signup forms, for branding purposes, then just use the **Embedded forms** option within the **Signup forms** sub-menu.

SUPERSIZE ME!

In book one of this trilogy, I talked about how UK author, Mark Dawson, used email marketing (among other things) to earn $450,000 in one year from his readership. In Anik Singal's book, *The Circle of Profit*, he discusses how he was able to scale his own "information product" business to $3,000,000 using similar strategies.

> The simplicity of this Circle is a gift. It is this very gift that allows you to focus on your life while letting the business run itself. You can use the following system to make $100,000 a year, $10 million a year, or even $100 million a year. I have no doubt anymore about the scalability of this system. (Singal, 2016)

What Anik refers to as an information product, we authors simply call a book or a blog. Other than that, the strategies used are pretty much the same:

- create an enticing opt-in page and drive traffic to it using the strategies discussed in books one and two of this trilogy;
- encourage these people to become email subscribers to your blog via that opt-in page by offering gifts or special offers of some kind;
- further engage with your subscribers through regular blog posts and a monthly newsletter that offer deals on books and additional items of value (some of which will be discussed in this chapter);
- personalize their experience to keep them interested;
- make sure they're aware of each new book you release and encourage them to buy;
- lather, rinse, repeat.

That's how you earn a profit at this over time—by growing your readership bit by bit every single day. You set everything up with an auto-responder and let it run in the background while you continue doing what you love best—writing! How perfect is that? I swear this whole online business world was built just for us writers. (Even Anik has a section in his book devoted to teaching other online marketers where to hire writers to help them create their information products. We're precious commodities, my friend! Don't ever let anyone else try to tell you differently!)

Now, there are some additional things you can do to scale your business even larger than you may have originally expected. Anik refers to this as building a $1,000,000 sales funnel:

> A funnel is a group of products that are strategically sold, one by one, to existing customers.

> For example, let's say you go to McDonald's and order a Big Mac. The cashier behind the register asks, "Do you want fries with that?" Then he asks if you'd like a soda, too.

> You were just the target of a small sales funnel: After you agree to become a customer by asking for a Big Mac, the company positions other beneficial and complementary offers in front of you.

> By adding French fries and a soda to your order (simply by asking you), McDonald's just doubled the size of your order. Multiply that by millions of daily Big Mac eaters, and just imagine what that funnel does to their revenue. (Singal, 2016)

This chapter is all about how you can design an automated sales funnel to sell more frontlist *and* backlist titles to your readership. You can use it to promote additional books in a series or other complementary products and services (e.g., online courses, a podcast, et cetera). You can even use this strategy to get loyal readers to sign up as affiliate marketers who sell your books *for* you.

Would You Like Fries with That?

The very first automated email your subscribers will receive from you, one hour after subscribing to your list, is the **Final welcome email** mentioned earlier. There's a good reason why I want you to personalize that email to include a sentence that reads something like this: "I'll also make sure you're informed whenever there are other special offers available for you to enjoy." It's because this sets up their expectation of receiving additional deals—so they're anticipating future emails from you. That way, they'll be more likely to click on those emails and open them.

Vary Your Automated Blog Post Notifications

It's important to vary the information contained in each blog post you write so your subscribers stay interested in the blog post notifications they receive from you by email. In book one of this trilogy, I gave you 10 easy blog post ideas to choose from.

- Some are different types of educational posts that teach your subscribers new concepts or skills, or that answer questions they may have recently emailed to you.
- Others are promotional posts that sell your new (frontlist) books/products/services and contain links to where each of these items can be purchased.
- And then there are the "insider" entertainment posts that share personal information about you and your

life, your opinions on hot topics, quotes that inspire you, et cetera.

When you get personal with your subscribers in this way, you'll get the best response from them in return. Why? Because they'll view you as so much more than a distant author of books they enjoy reading; they'll see you as a real person, maybe even a friend.

A new blog post category I incorporated this past year is my Blogging Progress Reports. I was inspired by Joanna Penn to share all my micro wins along the way, just as she did, so you can see my *true* journey to success as an author. I hope doing so makes it all feel more possible for you on those days when you're questioning everything. That's what Joanna did for *me* when she very openly shared her own roadmap to a multi-six-figure income on her blog.

But Joanna does so much more than just blogging and publishing books. She is where she is because she has created a sales funnel similar to what Anik Singal recommends. She's learned how to "add fries and a soda" to each of her orders with a podcast, YouTube video channel, online courses, et cetera. Visit her website, and you'll see exactly what I mean: https://www.thecreativepenn.com/.

Set Up Five Automated Backlist Emails

An easy way to sell your older (backlist) books/products/services is to automate five more emails that will be sent out to subscribers, roughly one week apart, following the **Final welcome email**. Try to set these up to go out on different days than your blog post notifications and monthly newsletter broadcast so you don't have any overlap.

In these five emails, you may want to:

- offer specials for the first books of past series;
- redirect people to important one-off backlist titles (e.g., I promote an important book I wrote a year or two ago, that is still relevant now, that answers people's most common book printing questions);
- and/or promote relevant online courses (e.g., I'm set up as an affiliate marketer with Udemy.com where I sell both my own and others' online courses about writing and publishing here: https://polishedpublishinggroup.com/sales-coaching-for-authors/).

How you design these emails will be critical since it's a little trickier to move a backlist title than a new one. You'll want to incorporate the five "psychological hacks" mentioned a bit later in this chapter, in The Psychology of Email Marketing section. Doing so will improve your success rate.

Invite Subscribers to Become Your Affiliate Marketers

Another effective way to engage your fan base is to offer them incentives to help you with the promotion of your books. You can offer a free copy of one or two of your ebooks to those who are willing to share a book launch announcement with their own social media networks. Better yet, you can show your fans how to register as affiliates with the ecommerce merchant(s) you're selling your books through. Once their affiliate profiles are approved by a merchant, they can then download customized affiliate links to your books that will track directly to their profiles, and they can share *those* links on their blogs and social media websites, or even via email at launch time. It's like having a 100% commission sales force working for you, no upfront investment necessary, as described in this post titled

"Affiliate Marketing 101: Part I" on the Acceleration Partners® blog:

WHAT IS AFFILIATE MARKETING?

Essentially affiliate marketing involves a merchant paying a commission to other online entities, known as affiliates, for referring new business to the merchant's website. Affiliate marketing is performance-based, which means affiliates only get paid when their promotional efforts actually result in a transaction. (AccelerationPartners®, 2014)

As the author, you don't have to track or pay for anything at all. These transactions are between the affiliates and the online merchants they registered with. At the end of the day, you'll still get paid whatever royalty percentage you would normally be paid for the sale of your books on each merchant's website, and the affiliate commissions will be taken care of for you in the background. It's a win-win-win scenario for you, the affiliate marketer, and the retailer.

Amazon Associates

Amazon's affiliate program is called Amazon Associates and it can be found here: https://affiliate-program.amazon.com/home. Through this program, people can sell everything and anything Amazon has to offer—not only books. The only issue I have with their program is that affiliates must register, over and over again, for each separate website (e.g., Amazon.com, Amazon.ca, Amazon.co.uk, et cetera) in order to sell things to people around the world. That said, they've recently implemented a new strategy they call OneLink (https://affiliate-program.amazon.com/onelink/) that allows you to combine all those sites together as one after you've registered on them all. Believe me, this is a blessing.

Before OneLink came along, if you included an Amazon.com affiliate link on your blog for people to purchase from, it would only work for the American buyers who made a purchase through that link. It wouldn't register as an affiliate sale for any of your other buyers outside the United States because, when *they* clicked on the link to buy the item, they would be redirected to the Amazon site in their own regions. To earn a commission from all the Amazon markets around the world, affiliates had to display separate affiliate links for every single market—and there are *several* so that was a royal pain in the butt. Luckily, OneLink has resolved that issue. Now affiliates only need to add one main Amazon.com link to their sites and the other international sales will be taken care of through it. This makes me a very happy affiliate marketer!

Kobo Affiliate Program

The Kobo Affiliate Program (found here: https://kobowritinglife.zendesk.com/hc/en-us/articles/115008616207-Kobo-Affiliate-Program) works much the same way. Although it appears their program is currently only available in six regions (e.g., Canada, US, UK, Australia, France, Germany) compared to Amazon's twelve regions (e.g., US, UK, Germany, France, Japan, Canada, China, Italy, Spain, India, Brazil, Mexico), this is a fast-growing ecommerce retailer that is quickly catching up to its competition.

You can also become an affiliate marketer for other Amazon products that complement your book series. And you can list your own affiliate links to these products within the **Confirmation thank you page** that automatically goes out to new subscribers rather than using the default option of redirecting them back to your website. Here are a couple of examples:

- **Fiction book series about vampires:** Redirect them to an affiliate link like this one (https://amzn.to/2FinsDa) where they can buy vampire teeth simply by adding the link into the content portion of the default email.
- **Non-fiction self-help recipes:** Here's a cool Fruit Infusion Natural Fruit Flavor Pitcher that might complement your healthy recipe series: https://amzn.to/2OoQPI5. You can use this link as your **Confirmation thank you page** URL rather than the default signup form URL.
- **Inspirational poetry to boost employee morale:** Perhaps this Success Gift Pen with LED Light and Stylus Tip would be a nice complement to your inspirational poetry: https://amzn.to/2FmUTVj. Again, it's your choice whether you add the link into the email or use it in place of the default **Confirmation thank you page** URL.

Setting up an affiliate profile—and encouraging your followers to do the same—is an easy way to earn passive income. You need only set it up once and then automate it by including it as part your **Confirmation thank you page**.

Another thing you can do to monetize your **Confirmation thank you page** is to redirect new subscribers to your Amazon Author Central page. This way, they're seeing all your books together and can buy them direct rather than buying someone else's product through an affiliate link.

Invite Subscribers to Become Your BETA Readers

In the traditional publishing world, your edited book is sent to a professional proofreader for a final once-over before publication. In the digital world, you can complete that final proofread yourself; or, you can do what some of today's entrepreneurial authors are doing to ensure that polished result we're all after. Authors such as Mark Dawson and Don Massenzio are combining proofreading together with a form of market research in order to sell more books: they're using their top fans as BETA readers. In his blog entry titled "The Importance of an Editor and Beta Readers for Independent Authors," Don Massenzio explains how using your own loyal readers as focus groups can improve the quality and enjoyability of your books for everyone:

> Beta readers are early previewers of your book that read through it after the editing process is complete. They look for story element inconsistencies and other elements of your book from the perspective as [*sic*] a fan and a reader. It's a good idea to pick a couple of readers that are big fans of your writing, but are not afraid to give suggestions. This process is like having a focus group or preview audience for your product that gives their opinion to you on a small scale before you release it to the relentless general public. Beta readers will spot things in your book that you and your editor missed such as inconsistencies in character traits, likability of your characters, and other intangibles. This is especially importance [*sic*] if your characters span more than one book in a series. You don't want to

publish a book in a series that has continuity issues with previous books. (Massenzio, 2015)

I've mentioned Mark Dawson throughout this series because he is a highly successful and business savvy author that was mentioned in *Forbes* as earning $450,000 per year selling his books online. Mark not only writes and publishes several books per year, but he also uses beta readers to improve each books' saleability come publication time. So, this technique is definitely worth consideration. It is a new take on proofreading that may well be the wave of the future.

> One of the practices that many Indie authors have implemented is an advance or beta team of readers who serve the author in a few very important ways in exchange for a free, advanced copy of the book. #1 - These readers help tighten up plot holes, errors, and oversights through feedback as they read the book. #2 - They provide reviews on Amazon and other retailers once they [*sic*] book is live on their platforms. #3 - They also can be a great source of encouragement and affirmation for the author. Mark's beta reader team was fairly large (over 700 people) and they were very active in this most recent launch. (Dawson, 2016)

It's up to you: hire a professional proofreader; proofread it yourself; or, use BETA readers to proofread your books. At the end of the day, the path you choose will depend on your budget and personal preference. But I *do* recommend a final proofread of some kind, however you get it done. It will polish your book even further than a copy edit does which should positively impact your sales in the long run.

The Psychology of Email Marketing

I recently came across an article by Bernard Meyer titled "5 Email Marketing Psychology Hacks to Boost Engagement & Sales." It's a great read about various scientific studies that were done to better understand people's behaviours and how each can be applied to help you design more effective emails.

> Implementing psychological hooks in your email marketing campaigns can not just boost sales, but can also help you skyrocket your engagement and brand loyalty rates.

> After all, understanding psychology allows you to guide your subscribers and customers to take the desired action. This helps you get better sales, but it also allows your customers to quickly see the value you're offering. (Meyer, 2018)

The five studies refer to:

1. price anchoring (displaying a significantly more expensive book beside your own on the same topic can make yours look more attractive);
2. the paradox of choice (segmenting your email campaigns, rather than sending "everything to everyone," will improve engagement by preventing the state of "analysis paralysis" that is created by too much choice);
3. the fear of missing out (creating scarcity or urgency with "limited time offers" can entice people to buy now);
4. the foot in the door technique (getting subscribers to agree to a smaller request, at first, will make them more willing to agree to larger/pricier requests later);

5. and reciprocity (taps into some people's need to give back to you after you've given them something for free).

I highly recommend you read the article (which is hyperlinked in the Bibliography section at the back of this book). Read the individual studies to learn more about how and why these techniques work, then keep them in mind as you design each of your emails.

Scale It Larger by Reinvesting

As soon as you begin to earn profits from this business system, you really should get into the habit of saving 10% of it into a "rainy day" fund and reinvesting at least another 10% of it back into your business. You can use some of this profit toward more PPC advertising to grow your email lists larger in your sleep. As you earn significantly more, you can also use it toward hiring a publicist to help you syndicate more of your content (as discussed in *The Author's Money Tree*). That's when you'll begin to see a more rapid growth rate and realize the true scalability of a digital publishing business.

But things will take some time in the beginning, hence the "rainy day" fund. If you expect some struggles right from the start, you'll handle it all much better and have that "stickability" R.U. Darby had to learn about the hard way.

Before success comes to most people, they are sure to meet with much temporary defeat, and perhaps some failure. When faced with defeat the easiest and most logical thing to do is to *quit*. That is exactly what the majority of people do.

More than 500 of the most successful people America has ever known told the author their greatest success came just one step beyond the point at which defeat had overtaken them.

Failure is a trickster with a keen sense of irony and cunning. It takes great delight in tripping one up when success is almost within reach....

[R.U. Darby] recalled, too, his mistake in having stopped only three feet from gold. "But," he said, "that experience was a blessing in disguise. It taught me to keep on keeping on, no matter how hard the going may be, a lesson I needed to learn before I could succeed at anything." (Hill, 1937)

Even if you run into any "fault lines" as R.U. Darby and his uncle did, never give up. Seek expert advice from the many successful people mentioned throughout this trilogy. And remember my own struggles that I shared with you at the very beginning of *The Author's Money Tree*. We've all been there, and we're a community of people willing to help you when you need it.

This system *can* work for you as it has worked for so many others before you. I'm absolutely convinced that it can work for non-fiction, fiction, and even poetry authors. This digital publishing age is the author's gold rush, and I hope you strike it rich! Good luck to you, my friend.

BIBLIOGRAPHY

AccelerationPartners®. (2014, November 5). *HOW DOES AFFILIATE MARKETING WORK?* Retrieved from Affiliate Marketing 101: Part I: https://www.accelerationpartners.com/blog/affiliate-marketing-101-part-i

Dawson, M. (2016, May 27). *SPF-013: Masterclass: A detailed look at a book launch – With Mark Dawson*. Retrieved from Self-Publishing Formula (The Self-Publishing Show): http://selfpublishingformula.libsyn.com/spf-013-how-to-launch-a-book-a-detailed-look-at-mark-dawsons-recent-book-launch

Hill, N. (1937). *Think and Grow Rich.* United States of America: Meriden, Conn. | Ralston Society.

Massenzio, D. (2015, February 14). *The Importance of an Editor and Beta Readers for Independent Authors*. Retrieved from Author Don Massenzio Blog: https://donmassenzio.wordpress.com/2015/02/14/the-importance-of-an-editor-and-beta-readers-for-independent-authors/

Meyer, B. (2018, October 3). *5 Email Marketing Psychology Hacks to Boost Engagement & Sales*. Retrieved from WebEngage: https://webengage.com/blog/email-marketing-psychological-hacks/

Singal, A. (2016). *The Circle of Profit: How to Turn Your Passion into an Information Business*. Retrieved from Lurn, Inc. (www.lurn.com): http://circleofprofit.s3.amazonaws.com/The_Circle_of_Profit.pdf

INDEX

ABOUT THE AUTHOR

So many people are publishing books of all kinds nowadays, and they need guidance regarding best practices with everything from writing to publishing to selling those books. I've made it my life's mission to help others navigate this mysterious business littered with acronyms and peculiar old-fashioned practices.

As a bestselling author and TESOL-certified sales coach for authors with 25 years' experience in the North American English book publishing industry (in both the traditional and contemporary markets), I can show you how to write, publish, and sell your book(s) using all the effective traditional and online tricks of the trade. Add my substantial advertising sales and marketing background into the mix, and you have a serious mentor in front of you who can help you achieve commercial success as an author.

If your goal is to produce a professional quality book that you can sell commercially, the team at Polished Publishing Group (PPG) can help. We teach authors how to write a book, how to publish a book, how to sell a book. Professional project management services are also available.

Visit my company website here:
https://polishedpublishinggroup.com/

Visit my blog here:
https://blog.polishedpublishinggroup.com/

www.ingramcontent.com/pod-product-compliance
Lightning Source LLC
Chambersburg PA
CBHW041715200326
41519CB00001B/171